A PLACE TO STAY

HOTELS OF THE WORLD

A PLACE TO STAY

HOTELS OF THE WORLD

PHOTOGRAPHY | Grant Sheehan

TEXT | Shelley-Maree Cassidy

PHANTOM HOUSE

ACKNOWLEDGEMENTS

Much thanks for their assistance and support is due to Robert Achten, Crispin Bassett, Katrina Bennett, Stefano Bigatti, Silvia Biaggi, Jean-Pierre & Elaine Bourbeillon, Wendy Cameron, Liz Cathie, Scott Cato, Shashi Bashi & Bina Chaddha, Jane Connor, David Cowdrey, Donna Cross, Caroline Cundall, Scott Kennedy, Suha Ersov, Elizabeth Robertson, Lauren Robertson, Richard Weston... and the swimming man in the Perivolas pool.

Edited by	Mary Shanahan
Designed by	Origin Design
Printed by	South China Printing Co, Hong Kong
Film stock:	Fuji Astia 100
Cameras:	Nikon F series

First published in New Zealand in 1999
by Phantom House Books, New Zealand
Copyright Grant Sheehan (photographs)
Copyright Shelley-Maree Cassidy (text)

ISBN 0-473-06147-3

CONTENTS

A PLACE TO STAY

YOUR TRAVEL LIFE HAS THE ESSENCE OF A DREAM. IT IS SOMETHING OUTSIDE THE NORMAL, YET YOU ARE IN IT. IT IS PEOPLED WITH CHARACTERS YOU HAVE NEVER SEEN BEFORE AND IN ALL PROBABILITY WILL NEVER SEE AGAIN. IT BRINGS OCCASIONAL HOMESICKNESS, AND LONELINESS AND PANGS OF LONGING... BUT YOU ARE LIKE THE VIKINGS OR THE MASTER MARINERS OF THE ELIZABETHAN AGE, WHO HAVE GONE INTO THE WORLD OF ADVENTURE, AND HOME IS NOT HOME UNTIL YOU RETURN. Agatha Christie

This book is essentially about homes away from home for the traveller, about places to stay - the accommodation and the destinations. Hotels have always played a major part in travel, whether the purpose is business or pleasure. Often scenes of great events, mystery, intrigue and romance are contained within their walls, as may be history, both individual and international. The hotels featured here all distinguish themselves as fascinating places to stay, although each is as disparate and distinct as its guests.

In the era of the 747 no journey is so long that it is still much of an adventure reaching your destination. Negotiating airports and fellow passengers are often the most arduous elements. A click of the mouse now brings instant virtual access to the world and its cultures; actually being there seems to matter less and less. So, does travel still serve to broaden the mind? The desire to see for oneself is unchecked. More and more people are travelling, and tourism is the leading global industry.

THE USE OF TRAVELLING IS TO REGULATE IMAGINATION BY REALITY, AND INSTEAD OF THINKING HOW THINGS MAY BE, TO SEE THEM AS THEY ARE. Samuel Johnson

Even in this age of instant information transfer, travelling involves mundane process - booking tickets, packing and labelling luggage, and obtaining travel documents. The journey itself may be a smooth uncomplicated passage, or one with frustrating delays, bad service, lost luggage and expensive transfers. It is with a sense of relief that the traveller arrives at their destination. You reach your hotel, and whether modest or grand, old or new, it will serve as your temporary home away from home.

On entering the hotel, it is the reception that makes the first impression. You are checked in, presented with your key and shown to your room. And so begins the experience, good or otherwise, that puts the stamp on your stay. The refuge of the hotel room, a cocoon to cosset the travel-weary. Does your room offer a view, is it quiet, the bed comfortable, the bathroom well fitted out? These walls enclose much of your travelling experience, and become your retreat from the unfamiliar world beyond, a private space where you can rest and regroup, free from observation and domestic responsibilities. Is it any wonder we expect so much of our hotel room?

The public rooms are the outer sanctum, the transitory spaces where encounters are limited, privacy may be respected but our need of company, sustenance and service is met. It is here that we expect the hotel to wrap its arms around its guests, providing a world that is enclosed but not entirely exclusive.

TRAVELLING GIVES ONE SOMETHING TO TALK ABOUT WHEN ONE GETS HOME... AND THE SUBJECTS OF CONVERSATION ARE NOT SO NUMEROUS THAT ONE CAN NEGLECT AN OPPORTUNITY OF ADDING TO ONE'S STORE. Aldous Huxley

Of course the truly great hotels go a step further. While they provide the care and comfort we hope for, they offer that extra quality not always realised for the most hopeful of travellers - a memorable experience. These are the hotels that go the greater distance, that have a special quality much sought after but finally matchless - their very own sense of style. Our aim has been to capture that elusive quality in this book.

The hotels shown here are an arbitrary and personal selection, chosen on the basis of their style and interest, not tariff. Others we would have liked to include were ruled out by space or time constraints. Still more are opening as this book goes to print. Other travellers have recommended their own favourites. Maybe another book, another time...

We invite you to indulge in the most enjoyable of travelling experiences - to vicariously venture into a variety of hotels and to visit some of the most interesting destinations. Whether it's the ultimate urban experience of New York, the unavoidably cool attitude of the Ice Hotel in Swedish Lapland, the geographical hotchpotch of Las Vegas, the serene Lake Palace Hotel in Udaipur or the sanctuary of Kyoto's Tawaraya Inn - 'bookmark' your choices for your next real, or virtual, journey. Bon voyage!

FOR EVERY TRAVELLER WHO HAS ANY TASTE OF HIS OWN, THE ONLY USEFUL GUIDEBOOK WILL BE THE ONE WHICH HE HIMSELF HAS WRITTEN... THE ONLY SATISFACTORY SUBSTITUTE FOR A GUIDE WRITTEN BY ONESELF IS A GUIDE WHICH IS COPIOUSLY ILLUSTRATED. TO KNOW THE IMAGES OF THINGS IS THE NEXT BEST TO KNOWING THE THINGS THEMSELVES... Aldous Huxley: Along the Road

The Ambassade Hotel stretches along the Gentleman's Canal

AMBASSADE HOTEL | Amsterdam | The Netherlands

In what is one of the world's great cities on water, the Hotel Ambassade is canal-side, a priority in choosing a place to stay in Amsterdam. Situated in the historical centre of Amsterdam on the Herengracht (Gentleman's Canal) the hotel has a peaceful setting slightly off the major tourist track. Yet it is close to good cafés, restaurants and bookstores, to the many museums, the floating flower market and shopping streets. Nearby is the tree-lined Jordaan area, an old neighbourhood undergoing a renovation renaissance, and on almost every street there seems to be an Indonesian restaurant, reflecting the legacy of Dutch explorers and spice traders who journeyed back and forth to what was once called New Holland.

The Ambassade is a medley of gabled centuries-old canal houses. On a charmingly small scale, the ten buildings are cobbled together as a hotel. Each is four or five storeys high, with steep staircases, twisting corridors, and low beamed ceilings. No designer drew this hotel up - it has evolved in its own eccentric way. The Ambassade has a literary tradition, reflected in names signed in the visitor's book. The hotel is apparently favoured by publishers and writers such as Oliver Sacks, Angela Bowie, Salman Rushdie and John Le Carré. No doubt many were on book promoting gigs in the city. There is soon to be a hotel library, to house the many books signed by the author guests.

The hotel is discreetly signed, and blends well into the essentially residential area. Despite being made up of ten houses, it is comparatively small, with none of its fifty-two rooms alike. This is an elegant individual and friendly hotel. The ornate breakfast room overlooking the canal serves a generous traditional Dutch repast. Because it is such a pleasant and spacious room, with white lacquered walls and two story high windows, it is better to forgo room service and eat here. The antique filled sitting room next door is a good location to enjoy a leisurely mid-morning coffee or an afternoon drink, admiring the old and ornate walnut clock with its moving fleet of ships.

Our room looked out over the canal. The large windows opened wide on the early autumn afternoon, letting in the still warm sun. Just above the street and heads of passers-by, the room had a gracious and welcoming feel, the atmosphere of a comfortable home. The bed was placed in an alcove, with table and chairs placed beside the window, adding to the impression of being in a living room. With a glass of wine and food bought from a nearby café, we sat and watched Amsterdam go by. The boat traffic along the canal is a reminder that this is a maritime city and major port. There was also a constant stream of cars and bicycles, and the sound of murmuring Amsterdammers headed for cafés, to visit friends, or going home...

At night, the city's bridges, illuminated by tiny lights placed around their arches, seem suspended over a void until a boat comes by with its lights on. The huge variety of boats range from the trim to the wallowing-noisy tourist craft, a wooden dinghy being rowed to a nearby restaurant, barges motoring by on business, homes afloat and vessels tied up by their owners who are refuelling at a convenient café...

The Ambassade's added water attraction is a massage centre with flotation tanks. It provides a pleasant remedy for stress and jetlag, and perhaps writer's block!

Think of an archery target and you have a bead on Amsterdam, laid out within concentric circles formed by its five main canals. The web of smaller waterways within brings the total number to 160 canals, the city claiming to have more canals than Venice. Traversing these watery barriers are 1281 bridges, negotiated by 550,000 bicycles, and even more cars. All claim right of way, pedestrians beware!

Hiring a bike is an option if you prefer your own wheels, but Amsterdam is a city to enjoy on foot. At night, uncurtained interiors offer glimpses of how the citizens live, contemporary versions of Vermeer's light-infused canvasses which captured everyday Dutch scenes in the 17th century.

Cruising the grand canals in a rented motorboat is a rather more elegant alternative to a two-seater water bike. Tourist boats provide a seaman's perspective on houses built along the canal banks by wealthy mariners during the prosperous age of merchant sail. Famed for museums focused on art - Van Gogh, the Rijkmuseum with its Rembrandts and Vermeers and the modern art of the Stedelijk - Amsterdam also caters to more down-to-earth tastes with museums specialising in subjects as diverse as trams, beer, sex and football. Something for everyone...

Original beams in Attic bedroom number 68

The Gable of the first house of the Ambassade's ten

The Café 'T Smalle, a short stroll or sail from the hotel

The modern and the medieval coexist comfortably in this very cosmopolitan city. Fans of architecture should see the quirky apartment complex of Eigen Haard (Our Hearth), on Michel de Klerk's drawing board from 1913 to 1920. The striking Science Centre New Metropolis by Renzo Piano rises like an ocean liner from the harbour and there is cutting edge design from the appropriately named radical Dutch architect Rem Koolhaas. Check out Architectura & Natura, a specialist bookshop at Leliegracht 44, for guidebooks on modern Dutch buildings.

Amsterdam has a 400-year association with diamonds (and other addictive substances!). It is also linked with tulips, which have their own fascinating history. As the Hotel Ambassade has a connection with writers, it seems fitting to mention two excellent books featuring tulips, one a novel, the other a history.

TULIP FEVER, BY DEBORAH MOGGACH (PUBLISHED BY HEINEMANN)

The Amsterdam of the early 17th century was immortalised in seemingly serene domestic interiors painted by Vermeer and Rembrandt. Moggach's book adds another dimension to the artists' canvasses. Set in 1630s Amsterdam, a typical renaissance love triangle draws a wealthy elderly merchant, his beautiful but frustrated young wife, and the painter commissioned to paint the couple's portrait. The artist becomes entangled in a series of emotional and financial speculations, including tulip-bulb trading, and the lives of the three central characters are utterly changed. The text is interspersed with 16 beautifully reproduced Dutch paintings, a novel addition to this work of fiction.

THE TULIP: THE STORY OF A FLOWER THAT HAS MADE MEN MAD; BY ANNA PAVORD: (PUBLISHED BY BLOOMSBURY, APPROPRIATELY)

A gardening writer, Pavord has recorded the bizarre history of the tulip in a massive book that is both scholarly and entertaining. Originating in Central Asia, tulips were transported to Europe by the Turks. In the 1730s the Dutch were overtaken by 'tulipomania', with single bulbs changing hands for the price of a house. Other countries including France caught the tulip fever. While the Europeans eventually regained their composure, the tulip's popularity now reaches out to embrace the New World. Pavord's book is illustrated with hundreds of full page prints of the stylish flower.

The Ambassade Hotel Herengracht 341 1016 Az Amsterdam THE NETHERLANDS	Telephone: +31 20 626 2333
	Facsimile: +31 20 6245321
	Email: info@ambassade-hotel.nl
	Internet: www.ambassade-hotel.nl

FORTRESS FRANCE

The Château de Bagnols does not fit the Cinderella version of a traditional wedding cake style castle. This is a fortress to be taken seriously, a vantage point built in the early thirteenth century to forewarn defenders of approaching enemy.

Conceived in the age of chivalry, the fortress may have a new vocation as a hotel, but it upholds the medieval tradition of hospitality toward visitors. Guests are welcomed through its portcullis, their transport tethered and tended to in the car park, rather than the former stables, converted as part of the accommodation adjoining the Château.

With towers, moat, and a drawbridge entrance, the Château de Bagnols is a triumph of restoration over ruin. Originally built in 1221 it is now one of the historic treasures of France. But it was left to moulder after the Revolution, and a decade ago it was a sadly neglected ruin, with leaking roofs, cracked walls, a home to a family of crows and surrounded by a wilderness garden.

Prince Charming may have come late but the fortress has been awakened from its long sleep to again become the great property it once was.

Traces of the avenues and bassins marking the axis of the old garden were uncovered in the overgrown orchard, enclosed by a stone wall punctuated with small round decorative towers. An avenue of limes follows the terrace walls and four parterres, planted with cherry trees, are sheltered by yew hedges. The restored grounds recreate the original gardens, which, like the Château, overlook the little medieval village of Bagnols and the hills beyond.

CHÂTEAU DE BAGNOLS | Bagnols | France

View of the Château from the garden

The entrance, with the courtyard beyond

A contemporary touch is the glass wall that allows a view of the sleek courtyard kitchen where regional specialities are prepared. The Beaujolais style of cuisine has been described by Elizabeth David as 'the most sumptuous kind of country cooking brought to a point of finesse, beyond which it would lose its character.'

Many meet for coffee or aperitifs in the Grand Salon, where they are spoiled for viewing choice - splendid wall paintings, and large windows offer views over the countryside and into the courtyard. When we visited, the room was decorated with massive bowls of peony roses, out of season at that time of the year. The elaborately carved Renaissance fireplace dominates the room, and at each side of the hearth, doors lead to tower rooms.

Staying here is well worth the expense, and the privacy and shelter found behind the castle walls has appealed to many wearied by fame. The Château is peaceful and perfect without being pretentious. Sitting on the terrace looking out over the gardens to the hills and valleys beyond is to be lord of all you survey, which one guest, Charles VIII of France, assuredly was. The King's visit in 1490 is commemorated by the royal coat of arms above the dining room's Gothic fireplace.

The hotel's 20 rooms and suites have been expertly restored and each has a different character. Antique beds are hung with period silk velvets and embroideries, and dressed with pure linen embroidered sheets fit for modern day royalty.

Preserved within the Château's massive walls are a series of striking wall paintings, examples of embellishments added in times of peace and prosperity. The earliest date from the fifteenth century. Many were hidden behind partitions, plasterwork and other modifications made over time, and were only discovered during recent restoration work.

The Château exudes history and grandeur, but these qualities never overwhelm the aura of comfort and sense of human scale. Its bucolic setting, the Beaujolais region in the east of France, has been compared to the Tuscany area of Italy. This though, is quieter and less well known. Rolling green hills are blanketed with forest and vineyard, and hilltop villages, picturesque châteaux, fine churches and farm buildings are constructed of the local honey-coloured stone known as 'pierre doree' (golden stone).

The Grand Salon with its Renaissance fireplace

The Bedroom of the Guichard D'Oingt suite

In the weeks of autumn, the vine leaves turn colour and the grape harvest is brought in at the famous vineyards that make up the Beaujolais wine trail. The fruit is picked by hand in the vineyards such as Fleurie, Julienas, and St-Amour; and the wines are drunk – with others produced by neighbouring Burgundy and Rhone – at the Château and restaurants in the surrounding towns which include St Paule and Villefranche.

A head start on decorating a more modest castle can be made in the Château's boutique shop, where customers may be tempted by a collection of more than five hundred specially designed items. This stock includes handblown French glasses inspired by an 18th century Burgundian design, furniture, silverware and Limoges porcelain. The charming pink and white uniforms of the housemaids are not for sale.

The Beaujolais countryside viewed from the terrace

The Château is open April through to January, and would provide a great retreat for Christmas. Arrangements can be made with the management to open during the closed season, should you wish to have a castle to yourself...

An old cart from bygone Bagnols days.

How to get there: Travel by fast train (TGV) from Paris to Lyons, and then by car to Bagnols; otherwise fly to Lyons or drive down from Paris.

Château de Bagnols	Telephone: +33 4 7471 4000
69620 Bagnols-en-Beaujolais	Facsimile: +33 4 7471 4049
FRANCE	Internet: www.bagnols.com

The Hotel Claris

THE HOTEL CLARIS | Barcelona | Spain

'A BALANCED DYNAMIC'...

On Spain's Costa Dorada, named for its golden sand beaches, is the Mediterranean seaport of Barcelona, the capital city of the Catalonian region.

Catalonia has a long and proud history of rebellion and independence, often setting itself apart from the rest of the country. It was from here that Christopher Columbus set out on his voyage of discovery. Today it is deservedly famous for its collection of extraordinary buildings designed by Spain's most famous architect, Antoni Gaudi, at the turn of the 19th century, as well as architecture from the 15th century.

Even the airport is stylish, a fitting entry to this design-oriented city, which mixes medieval, Art Nouveau and modern architecture, and was home to great artists such as Pablo Picasso, Salvador Dali and Joan Miro.

Behind the ornate 19th century façade of the Hotel Claris is yet another collection in this city of collections. The Claris has its own Egyptian museum on the mezzanine above the lobby, open only to guests. Here you can take tea and out-stare a small sphinx, inspect the mummies, statues and carvings and pretend to be a discovering archaeologist, all in the comfort of your own hotel.

The owner of the hotel has assembled this ancient collection. Senor Jordi Clos i Llombart is one of Spain's leading Egyptologists and the founder of Barcelona's Egyptology Museum, which houses the rest of his collection.

Behind the exterior of what was once a palace are cutting edge interiors, balancing classicism and contemporary design, typical of Barcelona.

The Claris has an expansive lobby in which guests may watch the world go by. Here, ancient mosaic fragments and marble toga-clad Roman busts are juxtaposed with contemporary furniture by Oscar Tusquets. The black hotel doorman, clad in white, is another chic trademark of the Claris.

The Claris foyer with mosaics and statues

Our room is reminiscent of a ship's cabin, with parquet floors, kilim rugs and intriguing antique pieces, modern furniture and relics. But few sailors would be used to rich colours of russet wood and purple and room to move on two levels, all of which make this such a stylish space. And the closest expanse of water is the generously sized open-air swimming pool up on the hotel roof, where a city centre panoramic view is a bonus.

Hotel Claris is in the heart of metropolitan Barcelona, only a street away from the most fashionable and gracious avenue in the city, the Paseo de Gracia. On the broad and tree-lined Paseo de Gracia are two of Gaudi's most admired and visited buildings – the Casa Batlló, and the Casa Milá (known as La Pedrera, the Quarry). It is worth the climb up to the Casa Milá's amazing roof, topped with giant surreal superstructures - chimneys and ventilation shafts said to have inspired Darth Vader's helmet!

These are but two of Gaudi's bizarre and brilliant buildings, which are often likened to massive sculptures. While highly original, his forms are functional - the free form architecture reflecting his belief in providing natural methods of ventilation. Curved lines in the interiors, incorporation of the outdoors, and living spaces with movable walls are trademarks of this creative architect's unique work. Now recognised as a visionary, Gaudi's ideas are compatible with modern architectural thought and the growing acceptance of the benefits of 'biological living'.

A mecca for admirers of Modernism, Barcelona has Europe's greatest collection of Art Nouveau buildings. Although the movement inspired him, Gaudi's interpretation was unique. A soaring sight on the city skyline is the spectacular sandcastle spires of his Church of the Sagrada Familia. Only one stone filagreed tower was complete when Gaudi died in 1926 but work continues, a hundred years since it was begun, on this evolving organic artwork. In the manner of the great medieval cathedrals, his church is still not finished.

After marvelling at the Gaudi buildings close to the Claris, sit at the bar of the nearby Replay café, drink coffee, and watch the parade of passing Barcelonans. Or visit the design store of Vincon, with everything stylish for the home from fabrics to furniture...

Barcelona's most famous street, La Rambla, is an amble from the Paseo de Gracia. The busy promenade leading down to the waterfront is edged with cafés and bars, dotted with seats, trees and newsstands. Its mass of flower stalls colour and perfume the length of the street. La Rambla continues to the Colombus monument honouring the Catalan discoverer of the New World.

Roof top pool

Storefront on the Rambla Avenue

Barcelona is considered Spain's culinary capital and it's here you will find one of the most spectacular food markets. Mercat de la Boqueria has been the central market in the Rambla area for 160 years plus. Ornate iron columns, buttresses and arches support a large covered pavilion, underneath which is the 500 or so food stalls. Few of the market's original Art Nouveau stalls and fittings are left, the most famous is Ramona's. With its bright stained glass signs, cast iron columns and mosaic tiled sides, it attracts many admirers.

A xuxo, a fluffy cream filled type of croissant sprinkled with sugar, is a delicious 'bad' breakfast. You can walk the damage off, checking out the cheeses, wines, meats, and fish. By now you may be ready to try a tortilla while appraising mushrooms, olives, herbs, salad greens... Then take a rest from this gastronomic onslaught at one of the tapas bars, with a glass of cava, the Catalan sparkling wine.

Another of Barcelona's treasured collections is the paintings of Picasso. The Museu Picasso is in the medieval Barri Gòtic (Gothic Quarter), with its warren of streets and plazas one of the city's most interesting neighbourhoods.

The Casa Batlló, façade designed by Antoni Gaudi in 1904, with its 'dragon-back' roof of green ceramic tile

Luckily, to enjoy all this and more, the days seem to last longer. That may be because meals are later - lunch between 1 to 3pm, dinner around 9 or 10pm. The late nights can be spent in the many designer bars and clubs.

For a restful daytime experience, spend time in the gardens of the Park Güell. Take a picnic, sit on the mosaic tiled benches on the great serpentine curving terrace and admire the ornamented pavilions of another inventive and original Gaudi legacy to this fortunate city.

| Hotel Claris Pau Claris 150 | Telephone +34 3 487 62 62 |
| 08009 Barcelona SPAIN | Facsimile +34 3 487 54 43 |

A view of the Marlborough Sounds

HOTEL D'URVILLE | Blenheim | New Zealand

This is one of the key viticultural regions of New Zealand, where the climate has been compared to Burgundy in France. Yet New Zealand's long narrow shape, which means that nowhere is more than eighty miles from the sea, provides a unique maritime climate. Most of the vineyards are in coastal areas, warmed by day with clear sunlight and cooled by sea breezes at night.

In only thirty years since the first vineyard was established, Marlborough has become the largest wine-growing region in New Zealand. Some thirty or so wineries have been established, growing grape varieties such as sauvignon blanc, chardonnay, riesling, and pinot gris. Red varieties such as pinot noir, cabernet sauvignon and merlot are also planted here. The soil types, abundant sunshine, long autumns and crisp cool winters have proved the right ingredients to deliver world class wines. Such is the quality of the terroir here that international wine companies have invested in the region, with Swiss, French and Australian labels staking out their own claims.

Built in the 1920s, the old bank building has been skilfully converted into a new use. The grand staircase leads guests upstairs to what was once a walk-in vault, and which now forms the central corridor that leads to the bedrooms. Now you can deposit yourself for safe keeping in this small nine-room hotel. The huge steel vault doors have been kept, complete with their original brass plaques and studs.

Whilst the decoration is eclectic, this is not a euphemism for a mess. Themed rooms are a trend in many hotels, as proprietors strive to differentiate their establishment from others to appeal to the often-jaded palette of the regular traveller bored with the standard hotel room look. The themes here are understated, often more of a hint rather than fully realised, which is a more elegant interpretation.

The d'Urville Suite: The classic lines of the d'Urville Suite recall
New Zealand's colonial days, with a nautical feel in the blue
panelling to the dado line, a brass ship's bell, charts and antique
maps. Drawings by the Astrolabe's resident artist line the walls.

The Colours Room: A blaze of warm red enlivens the entrance to the Colours Room. Bold contrasts of high impact colours on the walls and fabrics are picked up by glass ornaments. This is a high-energy room with a relaxing atmosphere.

Downstairs is the d'Urville wine bar and brasserie, with its much praised menu and young chef who uses the local produce and wines to full advantage, gaining the restaurant an international reputation. A patchwork of orchards and vineyards, Marlborough is described as New Zealand's gourmet's province, and is home to the famous green lipped mussels, farmed salmon and locally grown olive oil. During the long hot summer, guests can sit at tables in the open air surrounded by vines. And in winter, sampling the regional red wines in front of the fire in the bar is a welcome relaxation after a day on the slopes of the nearby skifields.

With its agreeable (more than agreeable actually) climate, the country's highest sunshine hours and an easy going lifestyle focused on wine, food and water, Marlborough is a tourist magnet. And the whale-watching capital of the world, Kaikoura, is less than two hours drive away for the biggest fish story of them all.

THIS REGION WAS CERTAINLY
THE ONE THAT GOT AWAY FROM THE FRENCH!

Kuba Room detail: The Kuba room is adorned with
old African ceremonial textiles and tapestries.
An old teak box displays small intricate carvings,
and colourful telephone wire baskets made by
Ndebele women.

How to get there: Fly to Wellington, then on to Blenheim, or by ferry from Wellington. For detailed information on New Zealand wines, visit www.nzwine.com

Hotel d'Urville	Telephone: +64 3 577 9945
27 Queen Street	
Blenheim	Facsimile: +64 3 577 9946
NEW ZEALAND	Internet: www.nzcom.co.nz/travel/durville

BLISS AT BLUMAU... RESTORATION OASIS

We appear to be lost. Our taxi driver has slowed, and is anxiously leaning forward to scan passing road signs. We can see his worried face reflected in the rear view mirror. Our destination is the Rogner-Bad Blumau; a Spa Hotel located one hour's drive south of Vienna. It is nearly dusk and our one-hour journey is in danger of taking two as we drive through yet another picturesque village - or maybe it's the same one! - in the lush green Austrian countryside.

The House of Art, House of Bricks and the main building

THE ROGNER-BAD BLUMAU HOTEL   Blumau   Austria

Suddenly a sign looms - Rogner-Bad Blumau - and our relieved driver swings his carload of stressed passengers up a long winding drive toward the hotel. But we forget our irritation with the geographically challenged driver when we catch sight of the hotel. Located on the hillside is a surreal collection of buildings that would make even Dr Seuss look twice. Pink castles with golden onion-topped towers, oval eye-shaped structures with grass covered roofs, multicoloured textured walls, and in the centre, a steaming thermal mineral water lake!

Colourful and decorative, this hotel façade strikes a chord that wouldn't pass for architectural critique, but we are immediately amused and pleased by the contrast between this perky, exuberant building and its neatly manicured and ordered rural setting. It's visual fun! And as we were to find out, the hotel is also a place for serious relaxation and stress escape.

Designed by Friedensreich Hundertwasser, the famous Austrian artist and architect, the Rogner-Bad Blumau Spa Hotel is an unparalleled visual experience and drawcard for Austria's spa district of Styria. The grassed roofs and the total absence of any straight lines give the impression that many of the buildings are growing out of the ground. Hundertwasser believes that 'the straight line creates speed, speed creates stress'. Perhaps this philosophy inspired our taxi driver's roundabout route.

There has been plenty of architectural criticism of both Hundertwasser and his buildings. The hotel has been aptly described as a gingerbread fantasia, and it is certainly a modern take on the baroque castle. However, as a friend once said, aren't we lucky it's there so we can criticise it! Since the Rogner-Bad Blumau opened in 1998 it has enjoyed high levels of occupancy, and is popular for weekend breaks, so it demonstrably works as a hotel - form has not triumphed over function here.

Once inside, relieved to have finally arrived after our roundabout taxi trip, we are welcomed by smiling, sympathetic staff. Our room key is a bright blue wristwatch, a 'key-bracelet', with the inscription 'a life in harmony with nature'. Wear this and a wave of the wrist gains entry to all the guest facilities. Much more harmonious and easier to find than a plastic key card!

A LIFE IN HARMONY WITH NATURE

'THE MORE DIFFERENT THINGS THERE ARE,
THE RICHER THE WORLD...'

The outdoor pool

I THINK THE ONION SHAPE MEANS
RICHNESS AND HAPPINESS; WEALTH, OPULENCE AND FERTILITY

Eco friendly bedroom 1502

Our room, high in the pink onion-topped tower, is spacious and quite plain. The interior of unvarnished wood and natural fabrics is certainly more sober than might be expected after the somewhat tipsy exterior. However, the sobriety is abandoned in the tiled mosaic patchwork of the bathroom! Whilst it has the requisite fittings and an efficient shower, its cheerful, slightly crazy atmosphere is rarely found in bathroom design.

From our windows we can see the large outdoor thermal spa pool with its silver sprout water jets. And we imagine we can hear the sea, which is puzzling, as we are in landlocked Austria. An inspection reveals a second, smaller pool adjacent to the main pool. Its wave-making machine is in full swing, sending crashing waves from one end of the pool to the other, to the delight of bathers enjoying the instant surf. We rise at daybreak to photograph the sunrise. Golden early morning sunlight filters through the low mist hanging over the hotel, and at the main entrance, a group of people is busy unloading a hot air balloon. In the distance, partly hidden by mist and trees, the gothic steeple of a nearby village church glints with the rising sun.

After choosing a healthy and hearty breakfast from the enormous variety on offer, we wander the tiled corridors connecting the therapy treatment rooms of the Holistic Health Institute. Guests traverse these corridors on their way to and from the various treatments, usually dressed in robes and slippers supplied by the hotel. This is a state of the art health spa as well as an architectural whimsy on a grand scale; delighting the eye and senses as it restores the spirit.

Many different stress-relieving treatments are available, from computer controlled water massage baths to advanced dietary treatments, but it was the music and sound therapy that intrigued us. Initially doubtful of its worth, we listened to the description of this therapy with raised eyebrows. The experience proved the better test. The therapy was developed by Wolfgang Koelbl, a holistic doctor, and it is unique to the Rogner-Bad Blumau. The recipient lies on a couch, which has an instrument like a xylophone underneath it. This is strummed, allowing both sound

Sound and music therapy

Hot air balloon with eye-shaped house and main building in background

and vibration to soothe the mind. Added to this are several layers of additional sounds, using instruments such as the monochord, Tibetan singing bowls, and brass gongs and a sound pyramid. Sound therapy was used in traditional Tibetan healing and by the Incas, and Dr Koelbl believes music is the path to the inner self. Cynical at first, we both rose from the couch feeling uplifted and relaxed, our heads ringing with the beautiful and unusual sounds.

The centrepiece of Rogner-Bad Blumau is the thermal pool with its restorative healing properties. Massaging water jets are strategically placed around the edges and at the centre of the pool, bliss for a travel weary body.

It is best to visit the pool at twilight, lying in the warm spa water and watching the sun go down before swimming through a short tunnel into the indoor pool. You can relax yourself even further stretched out on a chaise then eat poolside or amble on to a leisurely dinner.

The two restaurants serve great food and wine which say more about good living than the spa environment - and there are no watchful calorie-counting attendants disguised as waiters to catch you out!

Go to this 'oasis of wellness' to relax, recuperate and be amused by the witty environment. During our stay, we didn't leave the hotel and its immediate surroundings, but there is masses for the energetic or rest seeker to do besides just 'spa-ing out'. Activities include golf, ballooning, and horseriding.

Restored and inspired, we boarded a hotel shuttle van headed for Vienna airport. Driving off, my last glance of the hotel through the rear window was to reassure myself that the three day experience, staying in what may well be the world's first inhabitable work of art was not just imaginary.

QUOTATIONS BY FRIEDENSREICH HUNDERTWASSER

Wall of the House of Art

How to get there: The Hotel Rogner-Bad Blumau is located at Blumau, 120 kilometres south of Vienna, or 60 kilometres from Graz. It can be reached by either train, taxi or rental car.

For reservations:

Telephone: +43 3383 5100-0

Facsimile: +43 3383 5100-808

E-mail: resm@blum.rogner.co.at

Internet: www.rogner.com

MOONSTRUCK

...'HAND IN HAND, ON THE EDGE OF THE SAND,
THEY DANCED BY THE LIGHT OF THE MOON.' Edward Lear

THE MOTU | Bora Bora | French Polynesia

Fishing nets drying

Anchored just off-shore from the near-mythical South Pacific island of Bora Bora, is 'The Motu' - a special retreat on an island set apart. In Polynesian legend, Bora Bora is a sacred island, the first to rise out of the sea. Protected by a barrier reef and its blue crystalline lagoon, it is surrounded by a myriad of small motus - islets. It's from this that 'The Motu' takes its simple name.

The eternal lure of islands has drawn travellers in search of peace, quiet and isolation - or at least the illusion of it - to tropical arcadia such as this, from time immemorial. The soothing sound of waves lapping on the shore, or crashing on the distant reef, often lulls the stressed into a blissful state of relaxation and sleep. A stunning climate, spectacular scenery, and beautiful beaches - for sunning on by day and strolls after-dinner in the moonlight - are on the 'wish list' of island-holiday seekers.

Searching for a place to stay in Bora Bora for this book, we saw an artist's sketch of a new hotel in progress. Our inquiring fax drew this descriptive email response.

Dear Shelley-Maree, ia orana (hello)!

My name is Frédéric Lemoine-Romain, I'm the assistant of Denis de Schrevel (General Manager), we are both in charge of the two Sofitels of Bora Bora (Sofitel Coralia Marara & Sofitel Coralia Motu). As Denis is out of the island, I'm answering now to your fax. I can give you some of the following informations to help you :

- the Motu is a private and exclusive resort; with 20 deep overwater and 10 deluxe (built on the island) bungalows (total 30), around 60 persons max. living on this property

- the environnement of the Motu is really exceptionnal (natural coral gardens, small hill with tremendous and amazing vues (several all around), different plants, ambiance climate depending where you are on the island, facing the famous Otemanu mountain of Bora Bora (in the best angle vue), area of reproduction of the famous heron (protected or preserved area for us, this is also the logo of the Motu)...

The Motu - island in the sun

The frangipane flower

47

View from the Motu of Bora Bora's twin peaks

- for all those reasons we decided to developpe a specific concept to offer to our guests of the Motu :

1. Luxury and Sauvage

2. Simplicity and Authenticity

- Luxury: inside of each bungalow and in the communal area (materials used, furnitures...)

- Sauvage: outside of the bungalow considering the beauty of the nature (sea, lagoon, the island in itself, protection of the environnement, back to the nature for each guest, in a large majority coming from cities...)

- Simplicity: human size island (one hour walking round trip), where the communal area is the heart, for simplicity and comfort (welcome area, activities desk, lounge bar, restaurant in the same "grand salon", panoramic one, closed from each bungalow...)

- Authenticity: in a real Tahitian ambiance (local staff from BOB), with local roofs, kohu wood used worked by Tahitian people knowing this wood very well, some of the employees able to give a real traditionnal and authentic touch for the guests that looked for it (barbecue on the island, explanations of tradition...)

- As it stays a small hotel, we can imagine offering to those exclusives guests something more than a hotel: like personnalization of all the different services guests of the Motu, for us, exclusives guests, will have a direct boat transfer from the airport to the Motu (if possible, check-in in the boat). This exclusif resort is not built to accept children and please no noise for our exclusives guests. Overwater and deluxe have the same space (49 m^2 inside + terasse), but overwater have add in each a round glass floor for the vue, and a large sundeck (12 m^2) with outside shower + steps and ladder to go in the water. Deluxe bungalow, very deep overwater with sundeck open to the lagoon. 3 beaches, sunny, several spots to use in the nature for picnic, relaxing small local "fare", outside barbecue... - As it is an upscale, private, and specific place, we added a permanent coordinator in charge of the stays of the guests, for a real personnalization and quality.

I really hope that this e-mail will help you to confirm to yourself, that we could probably be in your next edition, as soon as you will visiting us, you'll be, I'm sure!!!

Please receive our tropical and sincere best regards.

Frédéric Lemoine-Romain
Executive Assistant Manager

Overwater bungalow 121

Bathroom of 121

Boats at anchor in the lagoon

We started packing immediately! And here you can see for yourself much of what Frederic described so well. For those who seek a temporary escape, this is an ideal runaway destination. The high cost of living the South Seas' dream here is a price worth paying for something to remember long after you return to the real world.

Reception and reading room

Classic kilim rugs on the stone floors belonged to Suha's grandmother, and his mother made the traditional lace curtains, enhancing the feeling of being in a private home. Like home, there is no restaurant or room service, but the breakfast room on the rooftop patio serves tasty breads, hard-boiled eggs, fruits and coffee. Sitting in the morning sun drinking coffee and looking out over the village and mountains beyond seems a valid activity for quite some time. For lunch or dinner village restaurants just a stroll down the hill serve excellent local food and wine. A short drive from Esbelli House is the Gulludere and Kizilcukur Valleys, known as the Red and Rose Valleys. These are a fantasy of pink sandstone shapes and erosion-formed gullies that glow orange and red at sunset, attracting busloads of tourists in the busy season to watch from the vantagepoint of the car park. The valleys are a stunning sight, better viewed without a horde of onlookers, but worth seeing whenever.

Rock houses at Uchisar

The Kitchen Room cave bedroom once an old kitchen, the oven now the wardrobe.

In this spectacular landscape, hundreds of cone shape rock forms have been gouged out over the centuries to serve as crude living accommodation, stables or churches. Doors and windows are often dozens of metres from the ground. On the valley's lower path, Ayvali Kilise (the Church of the Quince) is a cave church with wonderful interior wall paintings dating from the 11th century. Scattered about this stone wonderland are occasional vineyards and orchards where a farmer or two may be seen toiling away behind a horse drawn plough. No television aerials or telephone poles intrude on a walk through this timeless landscape. Along the track we find a café carved in the rock, with log seats to enjoy Turkish coffee.

Some kilometres away, we drive through the village of Uchisar where colourful roadside market stalls lie at the foot of a cluster of towering rock houses typical of the area. Still further on, we stop to look over the village of Goreme. The vista is a dazzling array of textural rock formations, the architecture mixing recent conventional rock buildings with ancient conical houses and churches. All are aglow in the gold evening light. In the distance, the call to prayer breaks the deep silence, adding an eerie soundtrack to an already fantastical scene.

The following day we are to go hot-air ballooning, our first experience of this mode of flight. Owned, operated and piloted by husband and wife Lars-Eric More and Kaili Kidner, the Kapadokya Balloon Company flies two hot air balloons from April to November. This excursion means a very early morning wakeup call to first confirm that the weather is right. The day dawns stunning and perfect for flying with gas. On our arrival at 5.30 am, the balloons are inflated. Within minutes we are airborne ascending quietly into the warm early morning light, standing in our cane basket lined with the local kilim carpet. As we climb, the sunrise etches long shadows into the amazing landscape. At two thousand feet I can appreciate the phrase 'putting all your eggs in one basket!' Feeling the breeze on your face as fresh air rather than a draught from aircraft air conditioning is far more pleasant, though you do feel a deal more fragile!

But we feel in capable hands, with our pilot in the same basket and happy to answer questions as she adjusts the burner above our head, and communicates with the other balloon and the ground crew. We descend to a few metres above the ground and pass so close to a group of apricot trees it is almost possible to reach out and pick the fruit before drifting lazily, dreamily up across the sky... Of course landing is a key issue of ballooning - what goes up must come down is a very apt saying, and there's no coming in for another try! The pilot has to get it right the first time. We are impressed by the perfect touchdown, the basket bypassing bumpy fields to drop neatly upright on the back of the Jeep's trailer. When I congratulate the pilot on the faultless landing, she admits it is the first time she has achieved a direct hit onto the trailer. Once down, the balloons are packed away by the ground crew while the passengers are treated to cherry juice, champagne and cake to celebrate the flight. "Ballooning is one of the most beautiful things you can do in your life," Suha had told us. We agree – flying over the stunning lunar-like landscape of Cappadocia on such a magnificent morning has added to an unforgettable experience.

Room 16, cave bedroom with fire place.

Balloon over Goreme.

"OUR LAST MOMENTS IN TURKEY WERE HAPPY ONES,

AS WE DISCOVERED ISTANBUL AIRPORT HAS A MASSIVE
FREE TASTING COUNTER OF TURKISH DELIGHT, IN EVERY FLAVOUR!

How to get there: We flew from Istanbul to Kayseri on Turkish Airlines (1 hour 30 minutes) Either hire a car at the airport or arrange through Turkish Airlines for a shuttle bus transfer directly from Kayseri to Urgup, delivered to the door of Esbelli Evi House.

Esbelli Evi House	Telephone: +90 384 341 3395
Urgup	Facsimile: +90 384 341 8848
Cappadocia	E-mail: suha@esbelli.com.tr
TURKEY	Internet: www.esbelli.com.tr

Kapadokya Balloons, Goreme.

Lars-Eric More and Kaili Kidner

E-mail: fly@kapadokyaballons.com

Goreme, Cappadocia, Turkey

EAU DE COLOGNE

You certainly can't miss seeing, or lose your way to, this hotel, the tallest building by far in the neighbourhood! The former water reservoir, once Europe's largest, has been transformed into a contemporary and intriguing hotel.

The water tower was built between 1868 and 1872 by an English engineer, but it was made obsolete by an underground watermain system laid in the early 1900s. During World War II the lower floors of the water tower served as an air-raid shelter, but the upper floors were partially destroyed.

In the mid 'eighties, plans were conceived to convert the neglected building into a hotel. After four years of reconstruction work, including the rebuilding of the top floors and inserting windows in the blind arches, the Hotel in Watertower opened to guests in 1990.

The architectural monument is a bricklayer's heaven, with old and new brickwork a major feature of the interior, most particularly in the reception. Eleven metre high brick pillars with steel connecting bridges suspended across the core of the tower accentuate the interior's feeling of height and optical illusion. Furnishings were prescribed by French designer Andree Putman, an appropriate choice for this ultimate recycling project since she has expressed a belief in design being redemptive and a goal of creating things that last.

For the tower's new vocation as a hotel, she has used a cylindrical theme for many of the furnishings – armchairs, wall lamps, occasional tables, carpets and door handles appear as whole or halved cylinders.

Counter-pointing the rich brown of the bricks are dark wenge wood, and a palette of vanilla and sand tones, with rich yellow and royal blue used on velvet covered furniture reminiscent of the art deco 'thirties.

The Hotel im Wasserturm in its park-like surroundings

The reception desks in a two-sided lobby are an amusing play on the round theme, with the two halves forming a mirror image, an unusual effect for the arriving and departing guest! Time whiled away in the relaxation-inducing bar, also semi-circular, can induce confusion as you amble back to your room, when one side of the hotel is the same as the other. In this case, seeing double is not always a result of drinking too much. But even the strictly sober may not want to look down as they walk across metal bridging to their rooms.

The two halves of one circle reception

The view from the roof top terrace circling the restaurant is spectacular, taking in the medieval and modern city of Cologne, its trademark twin-towered cathedral, and the river Rhine. The restaurant interior seems somewhat at odds with the rest of the hotel design, but the food is excellent and the vista no less so. On a clear day this is an ideal vantagepoint for a visual tour of the city.

The Wasserturm's location makes for quiet surroundings more typical of a country hotel than one close to the centre of a major European city. It is a handy refuge for anyone exhibiting or visiting the myriad of trade fairs hosted by Cologne, which range from fashion to photography to food.

If you prefer to stay sequestered in the tower, choose one of the studio rooms, which feel more like apartments. Whitewashed and spacious, they have great circular windows, screened to soften and diffuse the light.

The other imposing structure on the skyline is the Gothic Cathedral, which was begun in 1248 and completed in 1880. It attracts visitors and pilgrims to see its golden shrine of the Magi. The cathedral's distinctive spires are an enduring symbol of a city with many Romanesque churches. Other attractions are shopping in the Old Town, sailing on the Rhine River or visiting museums. The great variety of museums include one with Europe's largest collection of American Pop art, a Beatles museum, and the taste sensational Museum of Chocolate.

The Reading Room Study

The penthouse suite with grand piano, bar, great sound system, private garden terrace and open air hot tub is a place to feel like a visiting member of the rock aristocracy. It offers one of the best views of Dublin, across to the Wicklow mountains and Dublin Bay.

If you needs must get out and about, it is a short stroll to Grafton Street shopping, galleries, theatres, cafés, restaurants, clubs and bars, both traditional and contemporary. An impressive collection of contemporary design is on display and for sale in the Irish Craft Centre, five minutes walk from the hotel. The parks of Merrion Square and St Stephen's Green are the city's 'emerald islands'. They are lovely even on 'soft days', an Irish euphemism for rainy weather.

A bedroom view

The 'Celtic Tiger' can be heard as well as seen, with renovation and rebuilding underway throughout the city. In fact, there are more jackhammers and drills than you can shake a stick at, and new hotels, restaurants and bars open at a rapid rate in response to the growing number of visitors and locals. Ireland's economic success is founded on benevolent tax laws for overseas investors and European Union money. The mood of confidence and the country's positive international profile have seen many ex-pats return to their homeland to share in its new found pride.

When the sun goes down, this is a party town. Not much of the old Irish puritanism is here - Dublin has the youngest population in Ireland, and even the no longer young act it. The city stays up late to enjoy the 'crack', Irish for good times. The huge number of pubs caters for virtually every musical taste from folk through to contemporary. Many weekend 'riverdancers' who come to trip the light fantastic go home with a hangover they may not think so grand on Monday.

Visitors can retrace the steps of past Dublin writers on the Literary Pub Crawl, the best excuse for drinking and talking I've ever heard. Actors, not short of a well-crafted witty line themselves, guide the tours of pubs where many of the city's famous (and infamous) drank and claimed their inspiration. Soaking up 'culture' while testing the local beverages is an appealing combination even now.

For somewhere much quieter, no talking or drinking allowed, the Library at Trinity College is a booklover's dream, with its timber vaulted ceiling and reams of books. The university is also the guardian of the Book of Kells, the treasured 9th century illuminated manuscript of the Gospels.

Dublin was the focal point of the struggle for and against home rule. The General Post Office still bears the scars of the violent 1916 Easter Uprising, and it remains the favourite starting point for demonstrations. Also the site of the 1921 Declaration of Independence, the post office is on O'Connell Street, a broad avenue on the north side of the River Liffey, now seen as the less gentrified 'new' city.

In this city so many have written so much about, you can at least author a postcard to send from this imposing building. From the classic old stamp counter, I bought a set of Dracula stamps. The creator of the notorious vampire was Irishman Bram Stoker, and the special centenary issue marked the anniversary of his birth. The ghoulish stamps are my small but perfectly formed literary souvenir of Dublin!

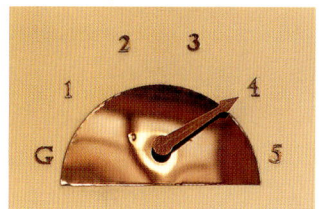

Lift detail

The Clarence Hotel	Telephone: +353 1 670 9000
6 – 8 Wellington Quay	
Dublin 2	Facsimile: +353 1 670 7800
IRELAND	
For information on Dublin visit www.ireland.com/dublin/essentials	

The Penthouse hot tub

The Ice Hotel at night, with the Aurora Borealis

Road sign

The hotel bar is open to guests and visitors. But lean too long on this bar and you'll be a permanent fixture! The Absolut Vodka company is a partner in the Ice Hotel, and its brand is of course the only vodka served. The other product placement is at the bar entrance; the opening is cut in the distinctive shape of the Absolut Vodka bottle. Beer is off the menu, as its low alcohol content means it would freeze in the cool atmosphere.

A post-nuptial party was held in the bar after a wedding celebrated in the beautiful ice chapel, where the seats and the bride were clad in fur. The wedding photographs gave the phrase 'freeze-frame' a new meaning. The newlyweds spent the first night of their honeymoon in the ice bridal suite. There are double sleeping bags.

On that same night guests were treated to an amazing bonus – the eerily beautiful spectacle of the Aurora Borealis. This luminous atmospheric phenomenon is triggered when particles from the sun collide with the earth's magnetic field. Here it is called the Northern Lights, and streaks of yellow, green, crimson and rose are painted across the starry Arctic sky as if some celestial artist is at work.

When it is time to chill out, guests are zipped into specially made Arctic survival sleeping bags designed to withstand temperatures down to minus 25 to minus 30 degrees. The warm under-layers you are sensibly wearing are kept on, and your outer-clothes stay snug in the sleeping bag with you. During the pre-retirement briefing, the guide advises sleeping on your back to avoid the possibility of your face freezing to the sleeping bag!

Lying in an all white ice bedroom, surrounded by a total and deep quiet, flickering shadows thrown by the flickering candlelight, is like being inside a snow cave deep within a mountain. The room temperature varies between minus four to minus nine degrees Centigrade, depending on how cold it is outside and the number of overnight guests - and you pay for this experience! Surprisingly, many say they slept soundly and warmly throughout the night.

In the morning you are woken with room service bearing hot berry juice. A traditional sauna lures, authenticated by the Swedish Sauna Academy, whose motto is 'in sauna veritas' - in the sauna, truth is revealed. Now you are conditioned to the chill factor, the steamy heat can come as a bit of a shock.

With a reconditioned thermostat, you can deal to a generous Scandinavian breakfast in the restaurant across the road. The cold air heightens the appetite for cuisine from the Lapland larder - game, berries, local venison and fish such as Arctic char.

The overnight experience can be extended with a stay in nearby wooden chalets, with full-on central heating. Daytime activities include safaris, with a team of ten to twelve huskies leading each expedition. There are more dogs than people in Jukkasjarvi. More than 900 sled dogs - Siberian and Alaskan huskies - are ready to take you on a fast trip through the Laplandic landscape of frozen lakes and snow-dressed pine forests.

Impatient to be off, the dogs bark furiously whilst waiting. Once they start pulling their load, they are contentedly quiet, and all that can be heard is their padding feet and the sound of the sled gliding across the snow.

Parking outside the Ice Hotel is for snowbikes rather than the usual cars. The bikes cover the icy ground more efficiently than any car, although the chill factor is vastly greater! Kicksleds are another mode of transport seen in the parking lot. This is a sort of wooden chair on metal runners, propelled like a scooter. Driving lessons quickly qualify drivers for both snowbikes and kicksleds, which can be used for short trips or longer expeditions to wilderness camps.

Now in its ninth year, the Ice Hotel has been a successful venture. Last year, nearly 4000 guests stayed overnight, while 20000 day visitors saw the massive snow and ice sculpture and enjoyed the adventure activities on offer in this stunning spot on top of the world.

Adventurers staying over in the Ice Hotel are presented with a certificate on their departure, as a permanent reminder of their igloo experience. They may have been comforted to know that the Cold Center, specialists in sub-zero physiology, was close at hand, in nearby Kiruna.

Jukkas AB	Telephone: +46 980 66800
The Ice Hotel	Facsimile: +46 980 66890
Marknadsvagen 63	
S-981 91 Jukkasjarvi	Email: reception@jukkas.se
SWEDEN	Internet: www.jukkas.se

URBAN RETREAT

The Tawaraya turns away from the street to face inward to privacy, peace and serenity. In a modern city with its share of urban chaos, tranquillity rules in this ryokan. Nearly three hundred years old, the traditional Japanese inn is dignified but not paralysed by the past.

The attributes of modern living are here but gracefully hidden, carefully shrouded in beautiful textiles or placed in containers that hide their form. You, honoured guest, also have your special place in this ordered environment. Other than a small and beautiful library that I'd like transplanted to my own home, there are no public spaces where you might confront other guests. Often, you encounter no one - even the staff seem to materialise rather than exist. Only room service food is available, but what food to stay in for! And there is the exquisite fussing of the staff, serenely mannered but ever alert to your smallest needs.

THE TAWARAYA INN | Kyoto | Japan

The exterior of the Tawaraya

The Reception

In a narrow plain street in central Kyoto you can take refuge behind the Tawaraya's walls, embrace solitude or enjoy companionship, contemplate, rest, be restored...

A pervading air of calm provides a sanctuary from the relentless race of contemporary life. Here are the real luxuries of silence, space and gourmet food - asceticism without sacrifice! Traditional Japanese architecture and innkeeping combine, providing a marvellous experience that is relevant and viable. Refined, luxurious, it is essentially a simple way of life, ordered and arranged.

Within these walls, the guest is the focus. You must submit to the routine and rhythms that are the ritual of staying in a ryokan. This is not an experience for those of harried temperament. Be prepared to adjust to the formality, the service and manners that are unlike any other style of hotel. Your role is that of honoured guest.

Having left your shoes and donned slippers at the entrance, you shed your travel clothes, and choose from the wardrobe of special kimonos and yukatas in your room. Slide back the shoji screens to contemplate the serene private gardens - with a stone pool where water flows from a bamboo faucet into the stone basin below, leafy maple trees and moss covered stone lanterns.

Rooms are simple, gracefully decorated with traditional style furniture, and some Western pieces for those who find it hard to sit on the floor. Traditional tatami matting is laid on the floor, sumptuous brocades cover the telephone and other reminders of the real world.

Your room is dual purpose, by day a living and dining room, at night transformed into a bedroom when a futon bed is made up for you.

The bathroom is an essay in contrast - you can soak and relax in a traditional Japanese bath, a deep cedar tub kept constantly full of hot water by apparently invisible attendants, or marvel at the high-tech toilet with its array of flashing lights and symbols, appropriately hidden from view.

The evening banquet looked too beautiful to eat. Visually stunning compositions are served by our smiling kimono clad lady-in-waiting who appears on soundless slippered feet, as if from out of the walls rather than through sliding doors.

Presented on exquisite Japanese pottery, each dish tastes brilliant. I start writing down a description of the courses for my gourmet cook friend. Several sakes later both my handwriting and descriptive abilities become blurred. I can no longer focus even with what must be the world's most beautiful hotel stationery and pens at my disposal...

Our ten-course dinner is cooked, arranged and served with absolute artistry. It culminates with a simple grapefruit jelly served in a grapefruit shell framed by its porcelain dish - a dessert that deserves to be enshrined.

This is followed by a deepest sleep in the softest futon bed... and then to be woken with morning newspapers and pots of tea.

Beautiful objects and changing table scenes in the corridors of the hotel reflect the seasons and events - May 5, horse racing; April, cherry blossom time; November, autumn leaves...

Room service

The Gyosuan (morning light) Room

Authenticity, or at least the illusion of authenticity, combines with luxury and service to harness past and present into a harmonious parallel.

Here you are surrounded by people who ease out the little inconveniences that make or mar the quality of life. They minister to the wants of guests with ceremony and elegance - service is an artform. Your lasting memories will be of the faultless manners that characterise this other-world Kyoto. That alone is worth the considerable expense. To be treated with such distinction, no matter who you are, invites mirror behaviour. A taste of old world courtesy and the opportunity to practise it yourself is another gain.

The Satow family has owned the Tawaraya Inn for eleven generations. Presently it is run, with gentle precision, by Mrs Toshi Okazaki Satow.

If you must venture out...

Kyoto is the ancient imperial capital, and it is here that the classic image of Japan survives. Behind the walls of the renowned temples, shrines, imperial villas and gardens is the traditional calm of Japanese culture. It hides behind the frenetic urban sprawl, with its traffic, neon signs, shopping arcades, crowded streets and pachinko parlours. The geisha quarter of Gion was the setting for Arthur Golden's book 'Memoirs of A Geisha'.

The Fuji Room from the garden - looking in at peace.

In the busy streets, swirling masses of young Japanese girls chatter and laugh into their tiny pastel cellphones, to each other...

The Ten-you restaurant, a branch of the Tawaraya is only two minutes walk for a tempura lunch or dinner, or there is the famous Kawamichiya noodle shop.

You will return to your refuge with a sense of relief, ready for its seductive shot of calmness and tranquillity in an otherwise frantic life. The ryokan's enclosed world is perfect for restoring balance after an excursion into this hectic city. A willing capitulation to the order of the ryokan encourages you to slow down, and surrender the tension you arrived with.

Departure is a ceremony in itself. The staff farewell sees the taxi out of sight, vesting the departure with such dignity you determine to return, to be treated again as the honoured guest.

How to get there: We flew into Kansai, one of the most orderly and attractive airports in the world, took the train directly from there to Kyoto, an hour's journey, and then a taxi to the Tawaraya. Alternatively, travel by bullet train from Tokyo.

The Tawaraya Inn	
Fuyacho, Oike- Sagaru	Telephone: + 81 75 211 5566
Nakagyo-Ku,	
Kyoto 604 – 8094	Facsimile: + 81 75 211 2204
JAPAN	

The Mosaic, entrance to the gardens of the Villa d'Este

THE VILLA D'ESTE   Lake Como   Italy

In the busy streets, swirling masses of young Japanese girls chatter and laugh into their tiny pastel cellphones, to each other...

The Ten-you restaurant, a branch of the Tawaraya is only two minutes walk for a tempura lunch or dinner, or there is the famous Kawamichiya noodle shop.

You will return to your refuge with a sense of relief, ready for its seductive shot of calmness and tranquillity in an otherwise frantic life. The ryokan's enclosed world is perfect for restoring balance after an excursion into this hectic city. A willing capitulation to the order of the ryokan encourages you to slow down, and surrender the tension you arrived with.

Departure is a ceremony in itself. The staff farewell sees the taxi out of sight, vesting the departure with such dignity you determine to return, to be treated again as the honoured guest.

How to get there: We flew into Kansai, one of the most orderly and attractive airports in the world, took the train directly from there to Kyoto, an hour's journey, and then a taxi to the Tawaraya. Alternatively, travel by bullet train from Tokyo.

The Tawaraya Inn Fuyacho, Oike- Sagaru Nakagyo-Ku, Kyoto 604 - 8094 JAPAN	Telephone: + 81 75 211 5566
	Facsimile: + 81 75 211 2204

The Mosaic, entrance to the gardens of the Villa d'Este

THE VILLA D'ESTE | Lake Como | Italy